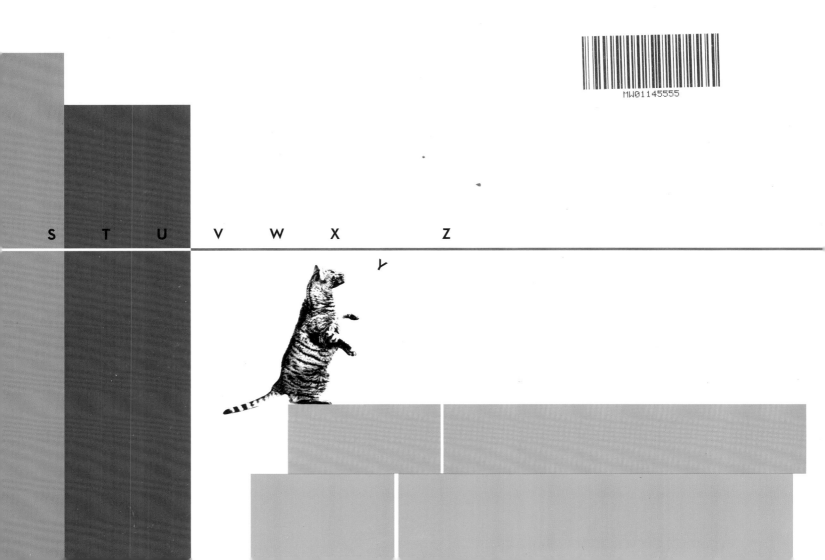

S T U V W X Z

THE
WELL-LETTERED
CAT

Dedicated to Taffy, who started it all

THE WELL-LETTERED CAT

PORTER EVANS

Design and Illustration
EDWARD FIERRO

LINES RAMPANT PRESS

Santa Barbara, California ™

Published by
LINES RAMPANT PRESS
P.O. Box 30731
Santa Barbara, California 93130

www.linesrampantpress.com

Printed by Ventura Printing, Oxnard, California, United States of America

Publisher's Cataloging-in-Publication
(Provided by Quality Books, Inc.)

Evans, Porter.
    The well-lettered cat / Porter Evans ; design and
illustration, Edward Fierro.
    p. cm.
    LCCN 2005905907
    ISBN-13: 978-0-9768837-0-8
    ISBN-10: 0-9768837-0-8

    1. Cats--Pictorial works. 2. Alphabet books.
I. Fierro, Edward, ill. II. Title.

SF446.E93 2005   636.8'0022'2
                          QBI05-600115

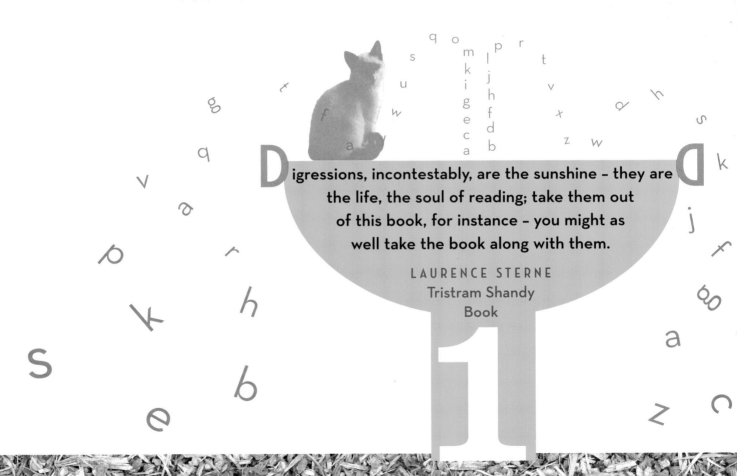

Digressions, incontestably, are the sunshine – they are the life, the soul of reading; take them out of this book, for instance – you might as well take the book along with them.

LAURENCE STERNE
Tristram Shandy
Book

appeared on a hot autumn afternoon. Although he wasn't Archie yet, of course – like all cats he would need some time to announce his own appellation. Nor, in fact, was it actually autumn, but rather one of those annihilatingly humid dog-days when August arms itself against the onslaught of September and Armageddon advances.

Accustomed though they were to the everyday alarums and excursions of an active family, the household cats sensed at once the alien's arrival and anticipated trouble aborning – always highly amusing. Abandoning all naps, they ascended the window sills with alacrity to assess the afore-mentioned Cat Who Would Be Archie, an amber tabby with amaretto eyes and an angular, avant garde frame, who was by now ambling around the azaleas.

Absolutely shouldn't be allowed in our yard, hissed Minnie the Agitator.

I think we should all roam free, replied Nicky the Anarchist.

I can take him alone, no problem, boasted Lizzie the Amazon.

2

Doesn't he look a lot like me? asked Reggie the Amiable.

He looks like you if you lost about 20 pounds, returned Magic the Abrasive.

But I can't see anything at all, wailed Sophie the Anxious.

And I don't *want* to see anything, whispered Merlin the Apprehensive, as he stuffed himself farther under the armoire.

3

All of you, this animus is unacceptable, announced Joey, an alphacat given to keen aperçus, and the amanuensis of this story. Wait for the Parents. But by the time they arrived, the alpenglow was fading into twilight, and Archie and a faint apparition near him – an edge of gray, nothing more – were dissolving into the ambient light like something out of the Hound of the

Baskervilles

But why had he bolted, the burnt-orange tabby? And who – or what – was his buddy?

Because Bonnie, a little tortoiseshell, had migrated from a home up the block, the Parents turned to her for counsel now. But Bonnie merely gazed beatifically into the blue beyond; being blind in one eye and quite deaf, she chose to see what she wanted to see and hear what she wanted to hear. In this behavior she was, of course, like all her feline kin.

Bedlam had broken out the week that Bonnie, then but a bronze-eyed kitten, had become part of the brood. Above a general ballyhoo in the backyard, two birds were circling; from beneath them came a series of

berserk cries. A crow baby had blundered out of its
nest in the palm tree and fallen onto the lawn below.

Believing they could bring up the fledgling, the
Parents built an outdoor structure to shelter him
during the day. Initially, the sight of the cat parents
approaching the cage to feed their baby would drive
the crow parents ballistic – the father would blaze
in bravely, bullet-straight, just over the Parents'
heads, while from behind him barrelled the mother,

a regular blatherskite, delivering a blistering beak-lashing. But eventually, the beleaguered twosome began to comprehend that these human forces were benign, and a trans-species brotherhood blossomed.

Behavior of the cats toward the little bird was surprisingly beneficent throughout his stay – even Minnie restricted her usual belligerence to a basilisk stare – and a particularly strong bond formed between Bonnie and the crow, the two babies of the family.

Bit by bit, Cornell the Crow grew stronger, until one day he was able to fly back to the tree to rejoin his birth parents. It was a bittersweet day for the household, but a very lucky one indeed for Bonnie, for the

Crow

was destined to do something quite extraordinary.

CORNELL GREW TO BE A COLOSSAL COAL-BLACK BIRD,

and the two families continued their cordial coexistence. For a time, he would come to the Mom's hand to eat, widening his capacious watermelon mouth to consume his favorite comestible: cheddar cheese chunks. But in due course, he ceased his childhood ways, and the Dad then constructed a fine custom bird feeder that lent the crow family's meals a certain cachet.

Complaisant Bonnie was yet a kitten then, and one afternoon, the Mom took her outdoors while she watered the flowers. After all, the courtyard was completely enclosed; what could possibly come to pass? And as the Mom made the circuit with the garden hose, Bonnie crept farther and farther afield, as curious kittens will.

CALAMITY CAME CALLING, ALTHOUGH THE MOM DIDN'T HEAR the opening chords over the cascading water. Too late the recognition of that cry – a hawk! Too soon the blood-curdling sight – the predator careening toward earth, beneath him the unsuspecting kitten, couchant. The Mom began running and calling, but Bonnie, deaf, only cocked her head and blinked back in her companionable way.

CAW CAW CAW: From the palm tree catapulted the three, the proud, the Crow Family. In closed battle formation, faster than a crack of lightening, they

dove in over the kitten's head and carried the hawk skyward with them, conducting him amid a crescendoing three-piece cacophony as far as the eye or ear could see or hear.

CRISIS AVERTED BY THEIR CHIVALROUS CONDUCT,

the crows were rewarded for their courage with, yes, a veritable smorgasbord of choice cheese products. And the cats, who admired the cunning of controlled timing even more than they did courage, celebrated Bonnie's rescue, too. All except Minnie, who had a competitive streak and could be quite a little

DICKENS

AT TIMES. AND WE'RE NOT TALKING ABOUT FLORENCE DOMBEY HERE, EITHER.

ELIBERATIONS OVER ADOPTING MINNIE HADN'T TAKEN LONG. HER REAR LEGS HAD BEEN BADLY INJURED AND SHE DESPERATELY NEEDED A NEW HOME. A PEACEFUL HOME. A HOME WHERE SHE COULD DESTROY THINGS AND GET AWAY WITH IT BY LOOKING DECORATIVE.

DECIDEDLY, SHE WAS UNHINDERED BY HER HINDQUARTER INJURIES. MINNIE (WHO HAD ORIGINALLY BEEN CALLED MINX, AND THE PARENTS SOON DEDUCED WHY) DEVOTED HER FIRST MONTH IN RESIDENCE TO EARNING A FAMILY NICKNAME: DEVILINA. THIS WELL-DESERVED SOUBRIQUET DERIVED FROM HER DEMONIC AND INDEFATIGABLE DELIGHT IN THE FOLLOWING DEEDS:

Dragging toilet paper from the roll

Digging her claws into sleeping scalps (human and feline)

Dealing sudden jabs from beneath the bed (may the devilina take the hindmost!)

Denuding every houseplant

Demanding food at 2 a.m.

Defiling all reading matter: books, newspapers, letters, bills. (Related talent: De-filing folders.)

Discipline, in short, flew out the window the second Minnie came in the door. (Other items also flew out the windows at times.)

"Decorum, Minnie, decorum," the Dad could sometimes be heard to plead

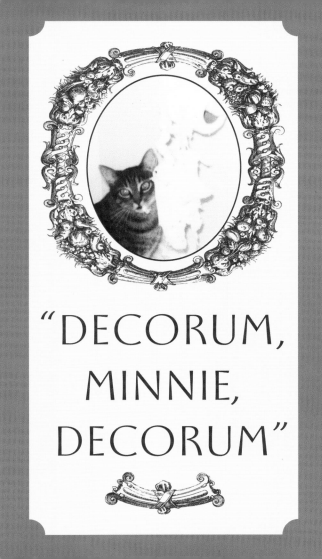

"DECORUM, MINNIE, DECORUM"

ABOVE THE MOUNTING DYSTOPIA. OF
COURSE, *THAT* MADE A HUGE DIFFERENCE.

ETERMINED TO PUT HER —ER—
DELIGHTFULLY OUTGOING PERSONALITY
TO WORK FOR A DECENT CAUSE, THE
MOM AND DAD ASKED MINNIE TO BE ON THE
LOOK-OUT FOR THE DISAPPEARING CAT.

OH, I'LL DELIVER HIM ALL
RIGHT, SHE THOUGHT, BUT I
WON'T DESCEND UNTIL I SEE
THE WHITES OF HIS

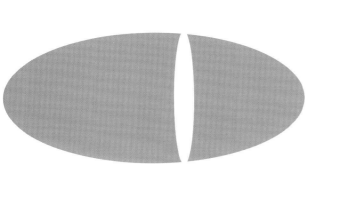

Eyes

Everyone knows, of course,

that when it comes to **cats,**

the **eyes**

have it.

Expressive eyes that epitomize eloquence,

enchant one moment and excoriate the next,

evoke effusive affection and eradicate all
woes with an elongated wink;

then eclipse those emotions with an
elegant show of ennui.

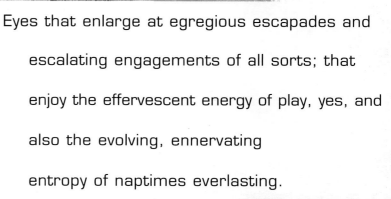

Eyes that enlarge at egregious escapades and

escalating engagements of all sorts; that

enjoy the effervescent energy of play, yes, and

also the evolving, ennervating

entropy of naptimes everlasting.

Eagle-eyed they were, and elaborate their
paths of exploration, but more time
elapsed and still they hadn't found the
orange ectomorph. Ensconced over
elevenses (crunchies) one day, however,
they had an epiphany:

It was time to call on Taffy, the

Font

of all wisdom.

First and foremost,

it should be noted that Taffy was, well, first. And foremost. And while the Parents couldn't see him anymore, the cats could bring him into focus as fully as ever.

Fair-haired and -minded, Taffy possessed, among many fine faculties, a fearsome mal ojo. One fierce look from him and any fracas froze; all folderol fizzled. And don't even try to get started on the fandango. Foolish indeed the feline who flouted mal ojo, and it never happened a second time. Whether they came into the family feral (Magic; Nicky), friendly (Reggie; Joey), or fey (Skippy; Sophie), each arrival fell promptly under his fell spell. And remained there forever.

TAFFY

From the beginning, Taffy had been the fiefdom's

DEFFENDER OF THE FAITH,

which comprised four articles as follows:

- **Food** : our favorites will fluctuate hourly

- **Freedom** : how'd we get out? we take the Fifth

- **Fealty** : FYI, as in human to cat, and not the reverse

- **Fraternity** : the Fourteen Musketeers – everything for us, and everyone for himself

Frustrated by their

failure to find the fleet-footed orange tabby – although fiery Minnie flounced, Frankly, I don't give a flying figment for that fragment of their imagination! – the felines fervently called upon Taffy for the real 4-1-1. They figured that with Taffy's fabled omniscience, it would soon be a fait accompli, as they say en français. But Taffy let it be known that he could only be their facilitator.

◼ ⅎFORTITUDE!

he added, as their spirits flagged and their faces grew forlorn. And before fading back into the firmament, he urged them to turn to Smokey, a real catus felis

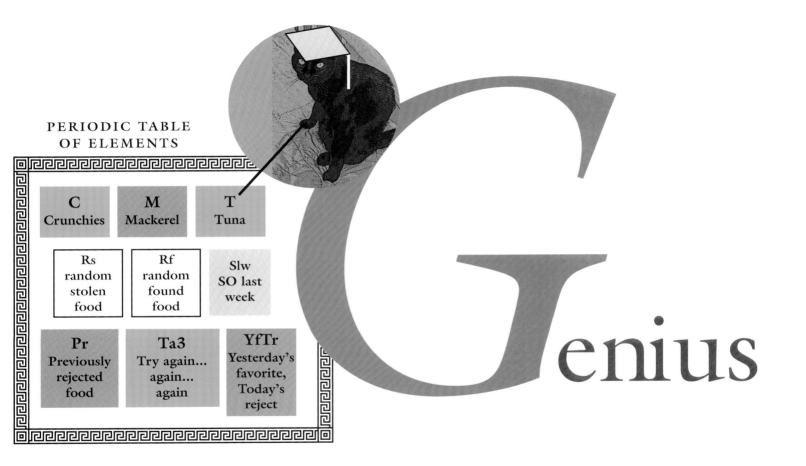

PERIODIC TABLE
OF ELEMENTS

C Crunchies	**M** Mackerel	**T** Tuna
Rs random stolen food	Rf random found food	Slw SO last week
Pr Previously rejected food	**Ta3** Try again... again... again	**YfTr** Yesterday's favorite, Today's reject

Genius

Granted, many felines are celebrated for their great intelligence, but Smokey, who may have had a Siamese grandparent perched in his genealogical tree, was a cat of gargantuan mental gifts.

Globe-trotting was Smokey's specialty. He had a way of getting *outofthegaragethrough thegardenandunderthegate* before you guessed what was going on. With his gregarious, garrulous nature, he ran the gamut from Gemeinschaft to Gesellschaft, and was greeted kindly everywhere.

Galvanized by the concern of the Parents, he waited until those two gadabouts were bringing in groceries one morning; then, gambling on their inattention, he gamboled right out the front door. The rest of the gang gazed goggle-eyed, and then began to chant:

GREEK CHORUS:
Go forth, Smokey, hither and yonder,
Travel the backyards of man.
Do not pause to worry or ponder,
If you can't find him, no cat can.

GALLANT SMOKEY:
Yea, I will look both near and wide,
Every shed, each cranny and nook.
I'll return with Orange Cat by my side,
Which'll make me the hero of this book.

Growing shadows betrayed the gathering
of night when next they glimpsed
Smokey, grinning as he trotted under the gate,
and with him came the thin ginger cat with
the gamine face and gnawed-on tail.

GREEK CHORUS:
Then gratefully the Parents cried,
And all were gladdened, of course –
Except for Minnie, gimlet-eyed,
Who growled, "Whatever goads your

G i

Hobbyhorse

y u p

Happily, there are many activities for the dedicated four-pawed hobbyist in this hacienda, enough to please the Uncle Toby harbored in all of us. Here, a few of the most harrowing household favorites:

Hieroglyphic interpretation: Lie across the Mom's notebook. Turn head upside down and study the strange marks. Roll leaky pen back and forth across paper surface until all is obliterated. This is known as "editing." When finished for the day, heave dripping pen into open handbag.

High-bunk hideaway: Assume position unobserved and feign a halcyon doze. Hammer on passing heads with claws j-u-s-t extended. Meet yelps of surprise with hazel-eyed innocence.

Extra credit for grazing the Parents' parts, which are widening noticeably, notes Minnie from her various withering heights.

Honing computer skills: Join the Dad when he's under a hectic deadline to learn more about the hilarious world of graphic design. Helpful assistance in the form of spit-polishing keys and tapping "Delete: All" is always welcome. While you're at it, change that humdrum screen saver to a glamour shot – you.

Harassing passing hounds: Hunker down on window sill with a hail-fellow-well-met expression. Emit glissando (hiss to howl) if dog approaches. Caution: May be hair-raising if performed in that window with the huge hole in the screen; you know the one we mean.

Hogging pillows: Start with corner of occupied pillow. Extend limbs. Push with all four paws. When the Parents react, leap as if stuck with hatpin. Accept their humble apologies. After a brief hiatus, return. Repeat until they are haggard, at which point they may arise and return to useful tasks, such as opening cans.

alloween was at hand and that, of course, is historically a hepcat heyday. In Archie's honor, all the hairy hoydens and hooligans huddled 'round for their version of a hedonistic hayride – conjure up, if you can, a kind of a Hieronymus Bosch scene crossed with an old-fashioned Festa

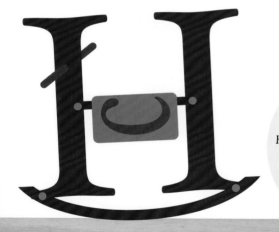

"So long as a man rides his hobby-horse peaceably and quietly along the King's highway, and neither compels you or me to get up behind him, – pray, Sir, what have either you or I to do with it?"

LAURENCE STERNE
Tristam Shandy
Book 1

Italic

It's time to celebrate!

Into the dirt!

Imbroglio!

In less than a tick, they were in it and at it:

gyrating, vibrating, squirming

all the while; now askew, then aslant, then practically asunder; with a wiggle and a squiggle, and a wave and a bend; with a tremble and a wobble, and a shimmy and a shake; undulating one way, leaning to the left; oscillating one more time and slanting to the right. Ahh. . .

Incredibile!

I just love a good dust-up!
cried Minnie the Instigator

I think you look more like a dirtbag,
said Magic the Inimical

Is this what they mean by true grit?
asked Lizzie the Intrepid

I hope it all comes out again,
worried Sophie the Immaculate

It always does, soothed Molly the Imperturbable

I know, let's go inside and jump on the white sofas now, suggested Nicky, the Iconoclast

Into the house they whirled like so many sandstorms, spreading filth to the couches! to the beds! to the keyboards!

Intently, Archie watched the other cats and, though he didn't join in, he did stop chewing on his infinitesimal tail tip for an instant or two. And bringing up the rear of all the insanity (and a dusty rear it was, indeed) was Everybody's Favorite Pal,

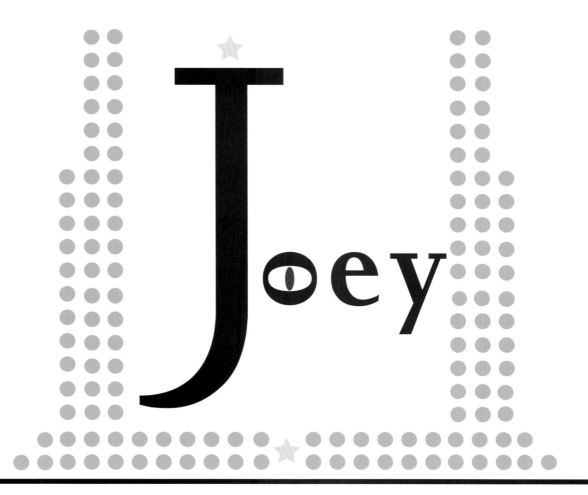

JUST AS TAFFY WAS THE
chairman of the board, Joey was the company's
CEO. More commander than admiral, more
bailiff than judge, Joey was not unlike Jeeves, as
he juggled the day-to-day demands of the fleet –
the court – the drawing room. Like Taffy before
him, he ruled justly, using the power of his
jocular personality and a certain je ne sais quoi
rather than physical force. But whereas Taffy had
the "eye," Joey had the "eek" – a high, jangling
meow that jarred the nerves and prompted small
nieces to joke, "There's a bird in his throat!"

Joey had been a jaunty tomcat with jewel-
green eyes, and he never quite lost the look of
the jungle – a mackerel tabby who fancied
himself quite the jaguar. Under his jurisdiction,
joining the clan was simple enough. Grabbing
prospective members by their jacka-napes, he
gave them a jovial stem-to-stern sniff-over and
indicated when they could eat (after he'd had the

juiciest bits) and where they could sleep (cheek by jowl, in any available jumble of limbs). Jeering at petty jealousies and gentling unkind jostlings, Joey brought a certain joie de vivre to the whole joint.

Jubilation at Archie's

arrival in the household was great, but the ensuing jamboree short-lived. One morning, jagged tears in the jerry-rigged window screen (yes, that one) told the story. Jettisoning other plans for the day, the Parents jumped into search-and-rescue mode. The English couple next door said yes, by jove, they'd seen him, jack-rabbiting past; a jogger led them to an orange cat who, alas, lacked Archie's white jabot. The crows were jolly well sure where he'd gone, but they weren't jabbering, while an old jay across the street delivered an incomprehensible jeremiad. By the end of the week, the jury was still out and the trial of finding Archie's trail had assumed

AFKAESQUE

PROPORTIONS.

Kittens, luckily, have been easier to assimilate into the family than grown cats (although there have been notable exceptions to this rule). Each time a kitten has signed on, an older cat has taken over its keeping, and, interestingly, the role of the kindly mother has always been played by one of the boys.

Keats's "goodly states and kingdoms" were kept in order by Taffy, so no one was surprised when he mothered a copper-colored stray kitten, Molly. Love was kindled as soon as the two of them were placed together on the

KITCHEN FLOOR. THEY WERE KINDRED SPIRITS JOINED AT THE HEART, AND SO THEY WOULD ALWAYS REMAIN.

KARMA OF KITTENHOOD HAD CONTINUED WHEN A NEIGHBOR BROUGHT OVER TINY, HYPERKINETIC SMOKEY. WOULD KOOKY MAGIC, WHO COULD BE A BIT OF A KILLJOY, FRANKLY, COME THROUGH? IN FACT, HIS CRANKY MOODS WENT KAPUT AT ONCE, AND CUDDLING SMOKEY WAS THE KEY TO HIS REFORMATION. WHEN THE TWO BLACK CATS NAPPED TOGETHER – A CONSTANT OCCURRENCE – IT WAS IMPOSSIBLE TO TELL WHERE ONE KIT LEFT OFF AND THE OTHER'S CABOODLE BEGAN.

KITH AND KIN TO EVERYONE, AND NEVER KINDER THAN TO KINDER, JOEY HAD TAKEN ON BLUE-EYED SOPHIE, THE WORLD'S MOST SKITTISH KITTEN. DESPITE HIS CLANGOROUS KOOKABURRA VOICE, JOEY SOON MANAGED TO GET HER ON A MORE EVEN KEEL, AND THEY WERE SHARING KIBBLE AND KISSES IN NO TIME. IT WAS TRULY KISMET WHEN SHY SOPHIE CAME UNDER JOEY'S CARE.

KVETCHES? MAYBE JUST ONE: THE BEAUTIFUL ELIZABETH (CALLED LA LIZ BY HER HUMAN GRANDMOTHER), WHO WAS BORN UNDER THE FIRE SIGN OF

refused to take an interest in any of the little ones, least of all Skippy, who was languishing for a playmate.

Leonine

Leonine was Lizzie, with her lynx-gray mane, lush white bib, and eyes of lucent lime green. A large girl whose own largesse extended principally to herself, she was no laggard at the dinner table – she especially loved lashings of cheese – and could eat the livelong day. Her leitmotif in all things, in fact, appeared to be "Lots!"

Literarily, her name was derived from Miss Elizabeth Bennett, and she shared her namesake's lambent wit. As a young girl, she had loads of feline admirers, but she rebuffed the louche and lovesick local tomcats as so many lumpen low-rent Lotharios. Loquacious, bodacious, and audacious, Lizzie vastly preferred the company of humans, her Daddy in particular.

Late one fall, however, she revealed that though she lacked a maternal instinct, she did not lack a mother lion's courage. One morning, just as it was getting light, Lizzie and Skippy were let out into the lattice-enclosed back patio. Several minutes later, the Parents realized that the backdoor to the enclosure had come unlatched during an overnight windstorm, leaving just enough space for two cats on a lark.

Launching into action, the

Parents first located Skippy, leg-locked in fear, looking toward the neighboring yard. The fence between the two homes had blown down, and there, just a few yards away, long fangs bared, loomed the neighbor's very alert and very large German shepherd. Luckily, he had not made a lunge for Skippy. And why? Because planted firmly between the two of them, all lustrous big fur, was that legendary beauty, La Liz. I laugh at danger! her stance declared. I could have you for lunch! The Parents didn't linger long, promptly returning both cats – Lizzie still livid – to the house. Praise and cream were lavished upon her in equal measure. (Well, more cream, actually, in accordance with her usual preferences.)

Languid and lively in turns, but

undoubtedly redoubtable, Lizzie, lamentably, never became the maternal type, but on that landmark day, she proved that when defences were lowered, you could count on her.

Leaping now to the opposite end of the spectrum of courage, one meets up with

Materializing mysteriously one morning, Merlin had evidently been meandering along more than a few miles of bad road and encountering his share of melees in the process. Covered with mites and matts, he had clearly found his journey through the metrop a bit de trop.

Meals must have been on the meager side, but once some minced meat and a bit of milk had been consumed, and the muck and mire had been combed out of his mane, he began to look more moussed than mussed. (What a munificent coat! the Mom would murmur. She enjoyed her own malapropisms so!) The new arrival bore such a marked resemblance to Magic that a mirroring name was chosen, and Merlin traded in the marginal life of the streets for the slightly more benign mayhem of family life.

Merlin's other meaning is black falcon, but if this Merlin – more meek than magical – were a bird, mayhap he'd be an ostrich. Once his magnificent head is immured, he fancies himself invisible, and in this make-believe appears to take much solace.

I will now disappear…

ABRACATABRA

I will now find Archie...

presto!

At the other, braver end of him, he brandishes a metronomic, meteoric plume tail, which he maintains in a vertical position, then whips menacingly side to side at a tempo meno mosso.

ourning still the missing twosome, Archie and his shadow, the family never imagined that modest Merlin could assist them. After all, neither Joey, the well-meaning major-domo, nor Smokey, with a merit badge in tracking, had managed it. (Mutinously, Minnie was secretly pleased, of course.)

Miracles happen every day though, luckily, and one November afternoon the Parents returned home to find Merlin asleep in a puffy mound against the screened back door. And curled up tightly on the other side, about one-quarter his size, dozed Archie. What had wrought the metamorphosis was never known, but he appeared finally ready to mingle with this madding and sometimes maddening crowd. Joey – as ever, a hardy Gabriel Oak – set a modality of cordiality, and he mentioned one day, It's time this guy had a

NickName

Skinny Legs

Skippy

Necessarily, he would require at least five, possibly ten.

For, with all due respect to T.S. Eliot, three names alone will not suffice. In this family, there are

La Sophine

A Comic Opera in Endless Acts

PERFORMED HOURLY

Names That Rhyme

Molly-nur-Nolly   Tabbs McNabbs
Smokey - Ker - Kokey

But Not All the Time

Francis   Demelza   Copper Penny

Nomenclature from Nature, Simple and Pure

Twiggy   Cloudy   Stormy

And Names That Are Simply Puerile

Fluffy-fluffums   Go-go boots   Skinny legs
Bristles   Moochie

Names from Kingdoms...

...Literary:
Elizabeth Bennett   the Brontë sisters   the Phantom

...Royal:
The King   The Queen   The Count   The Duchess   The littlest Princess

...and Animal:
the Bear   the Rat   the Penguin   Mr. Gorilla Mask   Pony Man

Nun, Wir Haben Katzenamen Hier

Liebchen   Hübschen
und also Merliner-Berliner

Et les Noms en Français, Aussi

La Sophine   Gigi   Le Fromage Petit

Good Dowager
QUEEN MOLLY
of the
Royal House
of nur-Nolly

Finally, the ne plus ultra –

NONSENSE NAMES

Goo-ey   Jangles   Mrs. Narnoosels   Mugglehead

Needless to say, it was no time at all before Archie became Archie-Kalarchie, Cookie dough, Butch cut, Sugarfoot... and that was even before the Parents started thumbing through the

Good morning madam, I'm Mrs. Narnoosels. The agency sent me; I understand you have a need for a gentle lap cat...

AKA Minnie

firm paw to run the place...

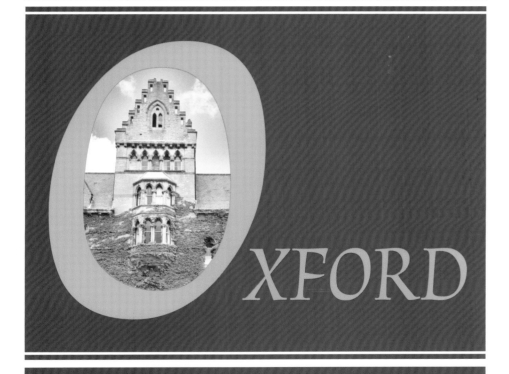

XFORD

OFFERTORY: A ceremony during which a small gift, especially of a deceased and saliva-drenched rodent or reptile, is deposited at the feet of the love object. May also be dragged under the beloved's pillow to express greater intensity of feeling.

OLD-BOY NETWORK: A telepathic communication system wherein cats advise one another of the Parents' imminent return home. Its verbal counterpart is the universal command, "Cheese it!"

OPEN-AND-SHUT: A centuries-old and still popular game consisting of waiting at doors to will one's Parents into opening and closing them. Points accrue based on the number of times per minute the Parent feels compelled to repeat the act during each turn.

ORATIONS: Exclamations connoting, "Oh, finally, some food!" The etymology is unclear. One school of thought traces usage back to ancient times, when cat armies carried the hated corn biscuits — referred to as "O" for "Other" — as rations. Some scholars believe the term may be a contraction of, "Oh, it's rat again," a comment heard frequently during informal barnyard suppers.

OTHERWORLDLY: A faraway expression, with eyes dilated and fixed on a distant and nebulous point. May convey disparate thoughts, such as "I'm bored now and I see an axe-murderer in the living room." Synonym: Opaque.

OUTLAST: A dangerous situation; a predicament to be avoided. Based on STATISTICS THAT INDICATE that the last cat out a door or window has the highest incidence per thousand of being caught again by the Parents.

Not to be confused with the saying "Out at last!", a battle cry indicating the regaining of one's freedom.

OVERFEED: A concept that is unheard of or irrational. Now considered obsolete, or at least, according to panel member Jude, obscure.

OMNIPRESENT: Most often used to describe Odin, the Norse god of wisdom and the creator of the cosmos, or his modern-day feline counterpart, Taffy, the family's

ONTIFF

WHO NEVER PONTIFICATED, LEAVING THAT TO THE PARENTS, AND WHO SERVED PEACEABLY AS THE FAMILY'S PHILOSOPHER-KING.

PRESUMABLY,

ALL CATS SHOULD BE PUSEYITES, BUT IN THIS HOUSEHOLD THEY ARE OF THE PANTHEISTIC PERSUASION. EVERY CAT IS A PUTATIVE GOD, AND WITHIN EACH CAT RESIDE ALL POSSIBLE GODS AND ALL THAT IS PURE IN NATURE. COMMON PRAYERS ARE THEIR COMMUNAL PURRS; THEIR VESTMENTS THEIR TRIBUNAL FURS. ALL ELSE IS POMPOUS CIRCUMSTANCE.

PALLAS ATHENA (LIZZIE) IS A GUIDING ANGEL, MARCHING THE PROPITIATING PARENTS ONWARD, ONWARD TOWARD THE KITCHEN CUPBOARDS. PLEASE PASS THOSE COLLECTED PLATES! THE PATIENT FAMILY PRELATE (JOEY) FAITHFULLY SHEPHERDS HIS FLOCK, PENITENT

q P

q P

AND IM-, WHILE SMOKEY, THE ALL-PUISSANT PANTHER, PANTOMIMES THE WAY TO TRUTH: OUTDOORS. VERILY, EACH CAT PREFERS TO WALK A SPIRITUAL PATH, ESPECIALLY IF IT'S A DAMP ONE THAT HAS JUST BEEN MOPPED.

PERHAPS ABOVE ALL ELSE, CATS SUBSCRIBE TO THE CONCEPT OF FELIDOMORPHISM:

DO NOT HUMAN FEMALES WEAR PLATFORM SHOES SO THAT THEY MAY PROPEL THEMSELVES MORE EASILY TO THE TOPS OF DRESSERS AND REFRIGERATORS?

DO NOT HUMANS PLACE SMALL WHITE BALLS UPON THE GREEN GRASS TO PERFECT THEIR MOUSE-POUNCING SKILLS?

DO THEY NOT ENTER INTO METAL SKYTOYS TO PURSUE BIRDS, MAKING, PRESUMABLY, A CHIT-CHATTERING SOUND ALL THE WHILE?

PONDER

THIS ETERNALLY PERPLEXING QUESTION AS WELL: WHY DO SO MANY MEN PARE OFF THEIR WHISKERS? HOW WILL THEY JUDGE WIDTHS OF PIPES AND PEWS, AND ALL PROPORTIONS SPATIAL, WHETHER PUNY OR PALACIAL?

POWERS HIGHER, CATS BELIEVE IN, BUT THERE ARE ALSO (SIGH) POWERS NIGHER. "PRESENT AND ACCOUNTED FOR" IS THE PARENTS' LITANY AT THE END OF THE DAY. DON'T EVEN TRY TO MAKE A PLAY FOR AWOL STATUS, BECAUSE YOU'LL ONLY HEAR, "HEY, BUDDY,

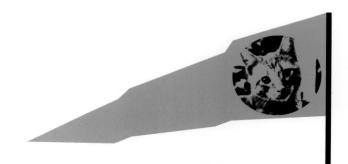

Quo Vadis?

QUO VADIS, TAFFY?

Quo vadis,
MollyMagicSmokeyReggieLizzieSkippyBonnie
JoeyNickyMinnieMerlinSophie? Archie?

Questions from the Parents — such quantities!
such quirks! — are uniformly met with
equanimity and smirks. Where are we going?
Anyplace that lifts us from the quagmire of
your quotidien little existence, for we cats live
and thrive on the qui vive.

Quenching our thirst for adventure

Quarreling over turf

Questing after quarry

~ Quoth Nicky, Magic, Smokey, and Minnie, the quartet with the quicksilver reactions and unqueasy stomachs.

Quavers Merlin, I'll just stay quietly inside.

Queenly Molly and exquisite Lizzie do not deign to answer their querulous Parents, nor does coquettish Sophie, whose unequaled azure eyes inquire, Pourquoi moi?

Quizzed, then, about their whereabouts, the cats quip, "Here 'n' thereabouts," and it's done without a qualm. Oh, we're quaking in our mittens, Mom, their unquelled glances say. 'Tis the quintessential clash heard in a quintillion homes:

Where did you go?

Out.

What did you do?

Nothing.

QUE SERA SERA, except that now and then, whatever will be, shouldn't have been. Despite the Parents' brusque warnings, quixotic quests are embarked upon, and the one in question took a queer turn and became known as the Story of the

REG AND THE BLACK

RESPECTFULLY, WE ASK YOU

to gather 'round as we recount the roman-fleuve of Reggie. 'Twas many and many a year ago, and many and many a mile away, when Reg chanced upon this family. A raffish, footsore kitten he was, thirsty, and flea-ridden. The Parents fed and bathed him well, and remanded him to goodly companions in the form of Magic and Smokey, who were close to him in age. But they rebuffed him, not remotely interested in the ruddy-coated ragamuffin.

Rudely shouldered aside by those who might have been his brothers, little Reggie made his own way in the family as best he could. Taffy and Molly, the reigning elders, made accommodations for him, but they were preoccupied with the rigorous education of the Parents and had many pressing requests to attend to. So although there was plenty of rich food to be had and many a soft bed to lie upon, Reggie made his meals alone and slept alone, and dreamed of a day when he would grow into his remarkably big feet, and go into the real world to make his fortune.

RIVERS WIDENED, MOUNTAINS TUMBLED, and Reggie grew. At last, the day of which he had been so long desirous was at hand. For lo these many weeks, he had watched the Parents moving between kitchen and garden, and realized that on rare occasions, they left the sliding door the tiniest bit ajar. So Reggie waited, recumbent, and one day, his courage bolstered by his curiosity and the ravenous consumption of an enormous lunch, out he stole unseen for realms unknown. And his rebellion went unremarked for some hours.

Rendered nearly mad by his disappearance, the Parents searched, reproached themselves, cried, rent their garments, and searched again. Relentless inquiries were made, and soon each tree bore a rough sketch of Reg and the word "Reward!" Nine long days came and went, and with them nine still longer nights, but naught was found or heard.

Resting on the tenth night – for real sleep still eluded them – the Parents heard a resounding meow ring forth. 'Twas their own dear Reggie's voice! And there he sat, outside the same glass door, roadweary and thin. They snatched him to their very hearts, and just then two more rascals emerged from the gloom: Smokey and Magic. Through means unknown, fair or foul, his big brothers had rescued Reg, after all. And the Parents never did know where Reggie had been, or how the black cats had gotten out, or how they had recovered him. To this hour, the riddle remains unsolved; but, suffice it to say that on that night was seen much rejoicing, and victuals aplenty, and that all were ready friends from that day forth.

ROUNDER GREW REGGIE IN THE FULLNESS of his years, becoming positively Rabelaisian, and his feet appeared diminished in comparison, giving him a look that was quite sans

SERIF

**S**velte as Reggie was rotund, Archie (the *other* orange tabby) soon felt right at home with the two sweethearts of the family: Skippy, a shy and silvery tabby, and Sophie, a sensitive snowshoe Siamese.

Skippy had survived the ways of the street, but he never grew street-wise. A scruffy six month old, he scooted inside one summer morning when the Dad was bringing in the Sunday newspaper, and he quickly became the spoiled baby of the family. The senior cats shrugged off his kittenish attempts at skirmishes, for which his opening salvo was a "Szzss!", succeeded by a look both surprised and sanctimonious. Magic did manage to sneak up on him sometimes, but Skippy was shielded by a general safe-conduct from Lizzie, whose substantial girth soon established a comfortably wide berth around the two of them.

Seven years later, Sophie moved from a cat sanctuary to, quite literally, the sanctuary of the family's sofa. On her arrival, she was so scared that she tried scrabbling her way into the side of the den couch, so the Dad sawed out a special space for her inside. To this stylish panic room she retired whenever society grew too overwhelming. Joey soon became her savior – and Minnie her scourge, but even their scrimmages became subdued in time.

Socializing Skippy and Sophie was a serious challenge. As with Austen's Marianne Dashwood, each cat's sense was swamped by sensibility. Both were so shy of strangers that every sound, however small, seemed Sasquatch squishing down the hall. Petting Sophie meant stretching your entire arm into the safety of her cubbyhole, until finally her silky head came forth to meet your searching fingertips. Of course, trust so hard-won is all the softer.

ophie and Skip may lack the sang-froid of their siblings, yet they are not sans insouciance. The term "sharp practice" is given new meaning for anyone who's been sobered by their saucy saber-tiger claws. They also share a tendency toward soggy salivary glands, whether suspended, dripping, over a scholarly volume, or straddling a sleeping face. Playing with stuffed toys in the sunny library is a favorite pastime, and they love scuttling small white catnip mice along the bookcases, as if casting so many pearls before Swinburne.

So there were several gentle souls on hand to welcome Archie to the household. Still, he clearly missed his sometime companion, and continued to chew, in Blakean circles of fearful symmetry, his skinny little

Tyger

tail.

TO EARN YOUR STRIPES IN A household where at any given moment you might have tails, nine, o'cat, trailing across your path, you have to learn to tread lightly. Those teasing tails are every-where: They spill along sills, drift down dressers, cascade from counters. Every twitching tail is a potential hair trigger, and an offhand touch can throw the entire family into a tailspin.

Tailey ho! taunts Minnie as she trawls the halls each day for tantalizing victims. Minnie relishes tailgating, and that's no picnic for the pursued. For a variation on her theme, she'll toss her own crooked little tail over the side of a table as bait, then quickly reel in the hapless cat-fish.

Tailanguage is a kind of international semaphore. Tails explode as the cats approach a blind corner (Courage!), then drop to level as they tiptoe around (Caution!), then spring upright again (All Clear!).

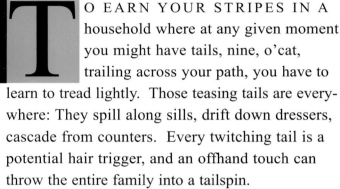

EM-DASH

CIRCA

There's tons of time to sleep in the afternoon, each tail tucked tidily around the nose and toes. The black cats twine together in their swallowtail coats 'til you can't make heads or tails of 'em, and torporific snores ensue. Yet whisper the name of any kit and that fitful tip will flick a bit. The troops may appear to sleep for hours, but their watchful tails are true sentries, always on duty.

TWILIGHT FALLS, AND THIS IS WHEN tall tales are told to the youngsters by Nicky, the grey eminence:

When I was a young Tom, I lived in the place of the towering oaks, and there the raccoons paid homage to me, and all of the birds, and even the Tyrannosaurus Rex, which one day slithered from the torrential river and is even now tromping toward . . . **You!**

Toward **us?** tremble the kittens, each on tender hooks, and their tails treble as they tread harder.

TILDE

The thirtieth nap of the day typically falls 'twixt midnight and three. Then, just before dawn, the traditional tribal beat begins – a drum tattoo on the hardwood floor. The rhythm of their lashing tails taps out a targeted message that is tried and true:

Get . . .them. . . up

Get them up

Getthemup!

T IRED-EYED, THE PARENTS TRUNDLE in. "What's the matter? What's going on?" they inquire with a tad of truculence.

Together, in a trice, a taileau vivant is struck. Noise? Who? Us?? (No tattletales they!) Tentative pink yaaaawns all 'round. . . . Tell you what, though, as long as you two are up. . .

Thanksgiving came and went, and there were special treats and much to be grateful for, but still no sign of Archie's shirt-tail relative, though they had cherchezed that chat through tous the

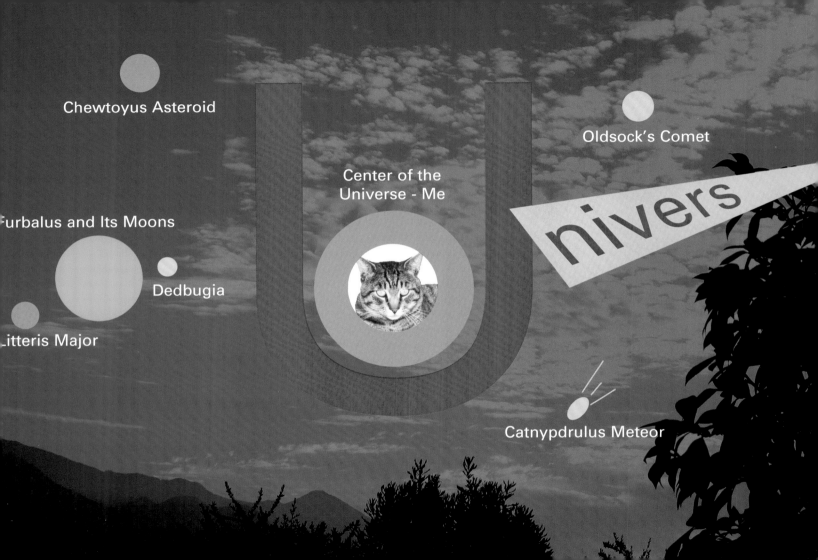

The Rings of Caturn:
Shredius, Pilowripion, & Drapeteria

Understandably, there was some consternation in the constellation when the gray cat did not reappear. Archie gradually settled in with his new family, began to gain much-needed weight, and even left off the nervous nibbling of his tail. Still, he often sat at the den window (whose screen – his portal to adventure – had finally been mended) gazing out at the rest of the cosmos with an unfathomable expression. And the November moon waxed and waned, and the trees put on their umber leaves, and the winter solstice drew near.

Unsurprisingly, little green-eyed men occasionally visit the home planet. The mercurial Minnie – not to be eclipsed by that Venutian beauty, Lizzie – at one point attracted a moonstruck admirer in the form of a neighbor's young Abyssinian. Minnie would lie along the balcony rail in seeming unconcern, while the Aby, a neophyte satellite, would make endless circles on the brick courtyard below. One day the Parents noticed that Minnie was focusing intently on something high overhead. With uncanny timing, she arced into the ultramarine sky like a plump, striped shooting star, intercepted an Unidentified Flying Owl in mid-air just as it was descending on the small Aby, and then landed (none too gently) on the rail once more. It is a well-balanced universe here, and, apparently, one in which even unwanted suitors are valued.

Unfortunately, as far as the Parents are concerned, the furry planets also manage the occasional orbit around the solar system. When the stars align – that is, when the Dad has his back turned, and the latch to the cat run does not click shut, and, most important, the Mom is on the phone, unaware – well, there are a few nanoseconds when an unruly astronaut has a chance to blast off from home base.

Satellite
Scoop-Able IV

Undeniably, there are many fascinating aliens inhabiting the greater galaxy. Nicky, the Überenegade, shuttles over to visit Callie, the long-haired calico next door, every chance he gets. She doesn't appear to

take umbrage and shares her lunch-crunchies uncomplainingly. Together they spend the autumn afternoons communing atop a tall stucco wall, their long comet tails undulating in the breeze, two good-time travellers in their own parallel universe.

Unfettered by fear, alas, Smokey and Magic once launched themselves into an entirely uncharted galaxy. By midnight they had still not splashed down, and the folks back at mission control were sending up urgent but unavailing distress signals. Suddenly, the two shiny black cats came rocketing down the sidewalk toward the home planet at supersonic speed, with two other four-footed beings – shiny black Dobermans – at their heels. After touching down in the foyer, the unrepentant duo requested dinner and then, unruffled, undertook a calm co-grooming session, undaunted by the gravity of their earlier situation.

Ultima Thule and Utopia have had their learned proponents, but still another dimension lies light years away. The stuff of urban legend, ruled by the Ur-Cats, it is known to humans as the

VoyagEar Space Shuttle - with propellers that can rotate in all directions or lie flat

and it's more than can be understood by the average cerebral cortex.

VORACIOUSLY CURIOUS, the Parents inquire, What is it, exactly? Is it a vacuum? Do you vaporize? Is it more like a virtual reality?

Vouchsafing nothing, the cats share with them the wisdom of Voltaire:

**Doubt is uncomfortable;
certainty is ridiculous.**

Vigorously independent vixens like Minnie and Lizzie set out for the Vortex with vim, on a whim, so the Parents suspect it may be a room with a certain va va voom. With bravado in his vibrato, Merlin will suddenly announce that he too is entering the Vortex. No, you aren't,

that's just a brown grocery bag, sighs Magic, vexed. (The rule is, in short, if they can retort, I'm in the Vort! – they aren't.)

VENTURING A LONGTIME question, the Parents ask plaintively, Where *were* you that time, Reg? Were you hiding...in the Vortex? His answering gaze is vague: Volo, non valeo, it seems to say. Sadly, the Parents fear that Taffy is lost to the Vortex forever, but he is merely veiled from their limited view. The other cats can always sense his presence with their special Vortex-Vision (for which Smokey is seeking a patent).

Veracity is Joey's forte so he valiantly attempts a report

on the Vort: Well, it's sort of like one moment, we're, you know, *here*, and then we do a weird thing with our eyes, and we end up, well, over *there*. Sophie, the shrinking violet with the valentine face volunteers, It's like, Voici! and Voilà! I've been there only once, but I can draw it – comme ça!

VIRTUALLY ALL THE CATS will vouch for one thing – vacationing in the Vort works up a powerful thirst. Like so many furry Volga boatmen, they row back toward the shores of home with verve in their hearts and a verse of "Yo heave ho" on their lips. For, as Voltaire has also pointed out,

**Anything that is
too stupid to be
spoken is sung**

On their return, therefore, they give voice to a few bars of the

song: (with a wave to Coleridge)

There's water, water everywhere
And every drip's for us.
We don't need bowls or nuthin' rare,
We lick! No mess, no muss.

Leaky faucets, those are best,
The shower curtains, too.
An auto hood can pass the test
With – yum! – sweet morning dew.

An overwatered plant is great
Because it's simply: FOUND.
For water is best tasted, mate,
Nigh wasted on the ground.

So spin on spigots here and there,
Don't rinse or fill or fuss.
There's water, water everywhere,
And every drip's for us.

When finally their song was done, the cats drifted down a river of reverie (like Coleridge's, steep and wide). Here is what they came upon (could one look, for a moment, inside):

> Mins was transformed to an albatross –
>> How she clung to the miscreant's neck!
> Bons took to wing with the shiny Cornell,
>> And he gave her an oh-so-sweet peck.
> Magic was dreaming of victory,
>> In the mud at Waterloo,
> While Merlin imagined a Fata Morgana,
>> Winced; was afraid to say "Boo!"
> La Sophine was visiting Paris,
>> Requesting, s'il vous plaît, de l'eau,
> And the handsome young man in the boat
>> on the Seine
> Turned out, bien sûr, to be Joe!

Welladay, said Queen Molly, as each came awake, thirst slaked and dreams half-baked. This is all wonderfully

-heighting, but now it's time to get ready for some exhilarating end-of-the-year festivities.

enophiles Joey, Smokey, and Lizzie were ecstatic about the excesses of the winter holidays. So many extravagant, chin-scratching people came to the house, bearing crinkly gift bags to explore, fresh excelsior to chase, and catnip toys to bury and exhume.

Xenophobes Skippy, Merlin, and Sophie regarded the inexorable approach of the celebration with a combined sigh of exasperation, then began preparations for their expected vacations by creating excavations under the bed, in the walk-in closet, and within the sofa, respectively. And each would then repair to his or her lair, exuding annoyance and waiting to exhale once the hols were over.

Xylography is an exemplary artform beloved by the Parents, and this year, fourteen little paw prints made up the family greeting card, with a message that exhorted: Paws Up for Pax.

(Minnie added hers under extreme protest, and only after an executive order from the Dad.)

Xylophone tones (from Merlin's basso profundo to Sophie's soprano) rang forth as presents were examined, giving a good vibe to the exciting proceedings. Magic received one of the few extant volumes to detail the exploits of Xerxes, while Minnie was given "Xanthippe: My Story," which extolled the virtues of excoriation. Reggie lovingly inscribed "Ex Libris: The Reg" within his dog-eared volume of "The Return of the Prodigal Native Son" and extended it to Archie, his fellow ex-wanderer. The collected works of Colette had been requested by Sophie, but alas, it was X-rated; the Parents gave her an expurgated edition instead.

Excalibur (an exceptional version in twine) was accorded to Merlin, who made a hasty exit back to his cave with it; and Lizzie seemed extraordinarily pleased with her copy of "Hippolyta, Queen of the Amazons: An Exculpation." Winding up the whole

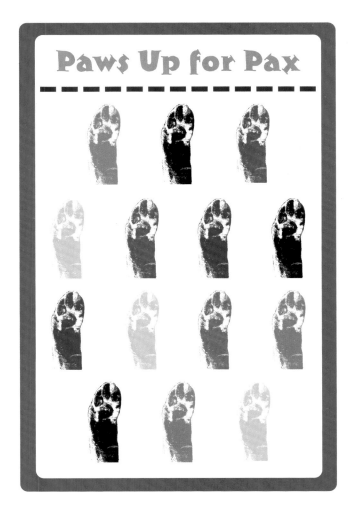

Paws Up for Pax

extravaganza, Bonnie received the original cast recording of "The Phantom of the Opera" – not that she could hear it, exactly, but there was an extremely close resemblance between her face and the mask on the album cover.

Xanadu, that's what this is, exclaimed Archie (for they were, after all, in a Coleridge mood) as all the cats in their jammers sat by the fire, exhausted by the gift exchange and an extensive period of treat consumption. Then, to their horror, the exuberant Parents gave a sudden exclamation and reached for that excruciating family

GO TEAM!

YEARBOOK

YIPPEE!

Congrats on winning the best all 'round – and we do mean round – award, Minnie!

YOGA

Bonnie, you're the mistress of feline flexibility in body and spirit. See you on the mats. Namaste!

YIKES

It took us long enough to find you, Archie. Enjoy your varsity position in the sun...you've earned it!

YUMMY

We'll never forget your trips to the unlimited salad bar, Sophie!

YOWZA

Maybe the Parents can't see you grabbing all the best gifts, Taffy, but we sure can. Always great to see you, anyhow. Happy hols!

CATIVITIES

YES, *it's been a terrific year, everybody. Remember to live by the school motto: Don't ever change your stripes.*

Yours very truly,

Skippy
Editor in Chief

Yawns are stifled (or not) and the Parents yield to an impulse to take one more quick walk around the block. In their hearts, they still hope that perhaps they'll catch a glimpse of Gray Kitty somewhere, but as usual they have

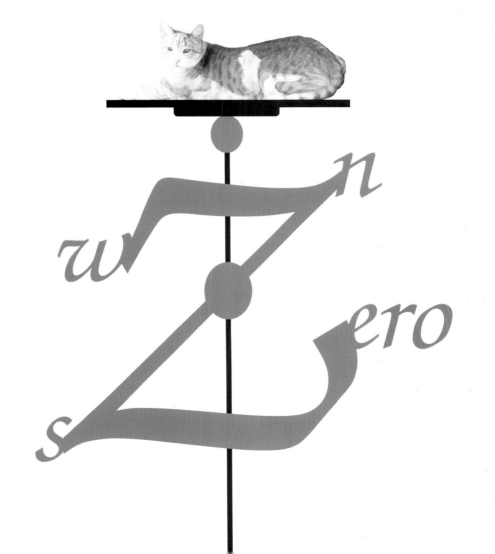

Luck.

Zeus, in the form of Taffy, tried to console the Mom and the Dad, but the general zeitgeist remained subdued. Zillions of fruitless trips around the neighborhood later, they finally began to give up hope of finding Archie's little pal. Zen was gradually returning – or at least as much Zen as can be had in the midst of a zoo – when one day there was a knock on the front door. There stood a middle-aged woman, smiling and holding a cat. And before Lizzie could say,

Zounds! or La Sophine could cry,

Zut alors!, the small silvery cat (for yes, it was Gray Kitty), leapt from her arms.

Zooming into the entryway, he careened around all available ankles before settling at his own mom's feet. The visitor explained that she had just bought the house next door, and that she and her two cats had stayed with friends in the neighborhood in the fall while she was househunting. When she was ready to return home to pack and move here, she couldn't find her second cat, an orange tabby. Was he here by any chance?

Zzzs coming from the den betrayed his whereabouts. The visitor looked in the doorway and found Archie zonked out amid his new siblings. "Well, he sure seems happy here with you," she said. "How do you feel about keeping him? And is it okay if my other cat visits sometimes? They've always been really close."

Zing went the communal family heart-strings! Amid squeals of some zeal (human and feline), the Parents zestfully agreed to this most welcome plan. After many professions of continued friendly relations, the woman picked up Gray Kitty and began walking away down the front path. A moment later, the Mom zipped after her, waving her arms in her zany way, and shrieking, "Wait, wait, what's your gray kitty's name?" "Oh, sorry, I meant to tell you," said the family's new neighbor, turning.

"Zachary."

W E GRATEFULLY ACKNOWLEDGE

the following characters,
whose frequent digressions,
typographic impressions,
minor transgressions,
and (rarely) confessions
have made this book possible.

THE FELINES

Taffy	Molly	Lizzie	Minnie	Merlin	Archie
	Skippy	Smokey	Joey	Sophie	
	Magic	Reggie	Bonnie	Nicky	

THE
FONTS

Avant Garde	**Joanna**	Sabon
Baskerville	KOLO	Times
Clarendon	Lubalin Graph	Univers
DONATELLO	**Modula**	Volta
Eurostile	**Neutraface**	Weiss
Frutiger	*Oxford*	**Xylo**
Galliard	PONTIF	YEARBOOK
Hoefler Text	Quant	*Zapf Chancery*
Isadora	RENNIE MACKINTOSH	

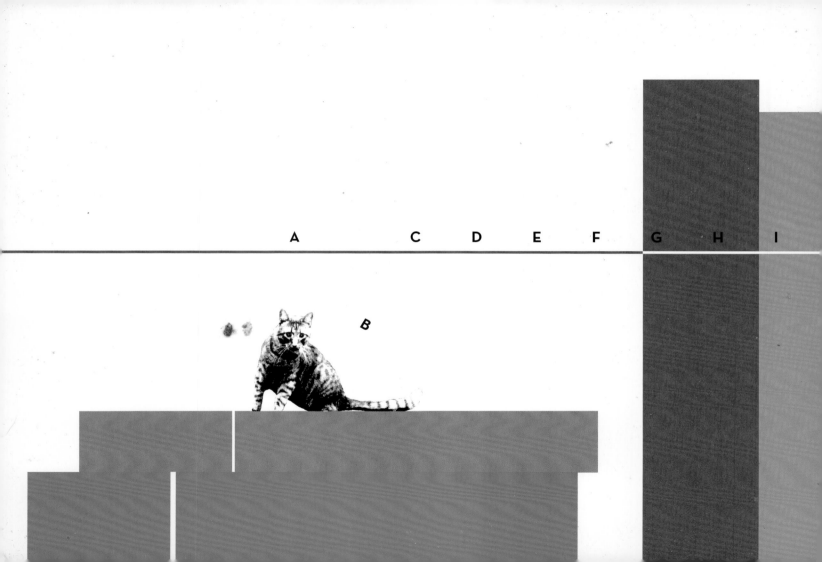

A   C   D   E   F   G   H   I

B